KING OF
BROKEN
HEARTS

GEORGE JONES

THE TENNESSEAN

IMAGES

To purchase images that appear in this book, see **http://tennessean.mycapture.com/mycapture/photoRequestForm.asp** and include the book's title in the description of the photo; or in the United States call 1-877-843-2900.

REPRINTS

To reprint or republish portions of this book, contact PARS International, **http://www.gannettreprints.com** or call 1-212-221-9595, ext. 116.

GEORGE JONES: KING OF BROKEN HEARTS

ON THE COVER: George Jones performs at Tennessee Performing Arts Center on Dec. 9, 1982. DAN LOFTIN

BACK COVER: Jones performs as part of the Musicians Hall of Fame Awards show at the Schermerhorn Symphony Center, Nov. 26, 2007. MANDY LUNN

Published by The Tennessean, Nashville, TN
www.tennessean.com/georgejones

ISBN: 978-1-4790-1005-9 (softcover)
      978-1-4790-1008-0 (hardcover)
Printed in the United States of America
Year: 2013

The Tennessean chronicled George Jones' life and career over many decades, and its journalists captured an enormous public outpouring of love and sorrow after his death at age 81 on April 26, 2013.

Jones' enduring popularity is a testament to music's powerful hold on our emotions. His life is proof that great talent can transcend flaws and trump fate. This book is The Tennessean's tribute to Jones and those who treasured the music and the man.

Country's King
of Heartbreak

No stranger to pain, George Jones delivered
gut-wrenchingly beautiful songs like no one else

By Peter Cooper
The Tennessean | April 26, 2013

"**T**he King of Broken Hearts" just broke many more.

Country Music Hall of Famer George Jones, a master of sad country ballads whose voice held the bracing power, the sweetness and the burn of an evening's final pull from a bourbon bottle, died at 5:33 a.m. at Vanderbilt University Medical Center in Nashville, Tenn. He was 81, and often called the greatest male vocalist in country music history.

"He is the spirit of country music, plain and simple," wrote country scholar Nick Tosches.

"He is the spirit of country music, plain and simple."

Nick Tosches, country scholar

George Glenn Jones was dubbed "The Possum" because of his marsupial resemblance, and later called "No Show Jones" because of his mid-career propensity for missing stage appointments. Those monikers seem trifling in comparison to "The King of Broken Hearts," which became the title of a Jim Lauderdale-written tribute recorded by George Strait and Lee Ann Womack. Lauderdale was inspired by country-rock forerunner Gram Parsons, who would play Mr. Jones' albums at parties and silence the room with an admonition to listen to the King of Broken Hearts.

"The King of Broken Hearts doesn't know he's the king," wrote Lauderdale. "He's trying to forget other things / Like some old chilly scenes / He's walking through alone."

Mr. Jones was well familiar with such scenes. He was bruised by alcohol and drug use, and in later, happier and sober years he wondered at the

ABOVE: Jones, center, entertains at the grand opening of his country music club, Possum Holler, on March 12, 1975. Jones intended the club, in Printers Alley in Nashville, as a venue for pure country music. NANCY WARNECKE

PHOTO ON PRECEDING PAGE: Jones, center, sings "Ragged But Right" to open a benefit performance at the Tennessee State Prison on April 20, 1976. DALE ERNSBERGER

"I think George is probably the greatest country singer who ever lived. ... All the artists loved him. The music just flows out of him. It's the most natural thing."

Cowboy Jack Clement, producer

adulation afforded him, given the recklessness with which he had at times treated his talent.

"I messed up my life way back there, drinking and boozing and all that kind of stuff," he told The Tennessean in 2008. "And you wish you could just erase it all. You can't do that, though. You just have to live it down the best you can."

The best he could was to sing about it, with an unblinking emotional truth that regularly rivaled and sometimes surpassed that of his own heroes, Hank Williams and Roy Acuff. He could offer a wink and a smile on quirky uptempo hits "The Race Is On" and "White Lightning," but he built his legacy with the sorrowful stuff. Betrayal, desperation and hopelessness found their most potent conduit in Mr. Jones.

"Definitely, unequivocally, the best there ever was or will be, period," is how The Village Voice's Patrick Carr assessed Mr. Jones' contribution.

Charlie Rich, left, Conway Twitty and Jones run through a dress rehearsal with host Eddy Arnold, right, for the second annual "Country Music Hit Parade" at the Grand Ole Opry at Ryman Auditorium in January 1974. DALE ERNSBERGER

"Definitely, unequivocally, the best there ever was or will be, period."

Patrick Carr, The Village Voice

Producer Cowboy Jack Clement, a 50-year friend of Mr. Jones who also has worked with Johnny Cash, Waylon Jennings, Dolly Parton and many others, said, "I think George is probably the greatest country singer who ever lived. And I'm not alone in that opinion. All the artists loved him. The music just flows out of him. It's the most natural thing."

Mr. Jones' signature song was the Bobby Braddock- and Curly Putman-penned "He Stopped Loving Her Today," which regularly lands atop critics' lists of greatest country recordings. In it, the King of Broken Hearts sang of a man whose death signaled the end of his unrequited love. In the studio, the song was difficult to capture, exacerbated by Mr. Jones' slurring of the spoken-word portion: When inebriated, he sang more clearly than he spoke. When the recording was finally concluded, Mr. Jones told producer Billy Sherrill, "It ain't gonna sell. Nobody'll buy that morbid son of a bitch."

But they did. Mr. Jones consistently credited Sherrill with the song's

Johnny Cash, left, and Jones, along with the Carter family, hold a concert at Tennessee Performing Arts Center on Dec. 9, 1982, to benefit the 100 Club, a charity for widows and children of police officers and firefighters killed in the line of duty. Cash and Jones first met on the "Louisiana Hayride" radio program in the early 1950s. DAN LOFTIN

Jones appears before a packed crowd at the RCA Label Show during Fan Fair at Adelphia Coliseum on June 13, 2002. RICKY ROGERS

success, but it was the empathy in Mr. Jones' voice that made the song's abject sadness somehow palatable.

"I'd rather sing a sad song than eat," said Mr. Jones, who sometimes lacked for food (he once withered to 105 pounds) but never for sad songs to sing. His treatment of those songs made him a legend, a designation that ultimately afforded him an uncomplicated satisfaction that capped a complicated life.

"That's what you live for in this business, really: to be remembered," Mr. Jones said in 2002, surveying the Country Music Hall of Fame and contemplating his place therein.

If Mr. Jones lived to be remembered, then his life stands as consummate triumph.

Jones performs at the grand opening of his country music club, Possum Holler, on March 12, 1975.
NANCY WARNECKE

GUITAR BECOMES LIFELINE

Born in Saratoga, Texas, on Sept. 12, 1931, Mr. Jones grew up hard. His father was an alcoholic given to drunken anger, but he bought his son a mail-order catalog guitar that turned out to be a lifeline.

"After my dad got me my first little guitar, I wouldn't lay it down, hardly," Mr. Jones told The Tennessean. "I took it to school with me. I'd hide it in the woods and cover it with leaves, and if a big rain came and it got wet, I'd pour the water out of it. Them guitars never warped."

By 15, Mr. Jones was playing and singing on the streets of Beaumont, Texas.

"A lot of them started throwing change down in front of me, down on the concrete," he said. "When I was done, I counted it and it was $24 and something, and that was more money than I'd ever seen in my life."

With his initial earnings, Mr. Jones went to a penny arcade, bought candy and played pinball. He married Dorothy Bonvillon in 1950 and divorced a year later. Mr. Jones joined the U.S. Marine Corps in the early 1950s. He was in the Marines when he heard of the Jan. 1, 1953, death of Hank Williams. Mr. Jones wept in the barracks to hear of the demise of his hero.

"The guy in the bunk next to mine (when I was in the service) showed me the front page of the newspaper with a headline that screamed that country music's greatest singer-songwriter had been found dead in the back of a car on the way to a show in Canton, Ohio," said Mr. Jones, quoted in the liner notes to the boxed set "The Complete Hank Williams."

"That sounded as far away to me as Europe, and I couldn't believe that someone who was so close to my heart had died in such a distant land. Music was the biggest part of my life, and Hank Williams had been my biggest

OPPOSITE PAGE: Jones lights into "No Show Jones," kicking off his performance as part of the Starwood Amphitheatre concert in Nashville on July 24, 1987, also starring Merle Haggard. More than 12,000 fans turned out for a night of music by the country legends. PEYTON HOGE

ABOVE: Randy Travis introduces Jones as one of the newest members of the Country Music Hall of Fame during the Country Music Association Awards show on Sept. 30, 1992. MIKE DUBOSE

OPPOSITE PAGE: Jones performs during Fan Fair at the Tennessee State Fairgrounds on June 11, 1991. KATS BARRY

musical influence. By that thinking, you could say he was the biggest part of my life at that time. That's how personally I took him and his songs ... I lay there and bawled."

In 1954, Mr. Jones was out of the Marines. He embarked on a recording career, making records for the Texas-based Starday label. On Starday, Mr. Jones scored his first top five hit, "Why Baby Why," in 1955. He soon began recording in Nashville for Mercury Records, where he notched his first chart-topping hit, 1959's "White Lightning," along with notables "Color of the Blues," "Tender Years" and "Who Shot Sam."

"['She Thinks I Still Care'] perfectly represented Jones at the time, his vocal flawless and keening, drilling hard on certain lines and lyrics for all they were worth."

Rich Kienzle, music critic

Mr. Jones moved to United Artists Records in 1962, scoring a No. 1 hit with his first United Artists recording, a Dickey Lee song pitched to him by Clement called "She Thinks I Still Care."

"The song perfectly represented Jones at the time, his vocal flawless and keening, drilling hard on certain lines and lyrics for all they were worth," wrote author and music critic Rich Kienzle in the liner notes of a Bear Family Records boxed set that includes Mr. Jones' recordings from 1962 through 1964.

For United Artists, Mr. Jones recorded other notables, including "You Comb Her Hair," "The Race Is On" and "Least of All." He and then-manager and producer Pappy Daily moved on to Musicor Records in 1965 and cut major hits including "Walk Through This World With Me," "If My Heart Had Windows" and the devastating "A Good Year for the Roses."

In 1968, Mr. Jones and his second wife, Shirley Ann Corley, divorced after 14 years of marriage. A year later, he married singer Tammy Wynette.

Tammy Wynette, left, and Jones chat with Merle Haggard and Bonnie Owens during the BMI Awards banquet at the Belle Meade Country Club on Oct. 16, 1973. ROBERT JOHNSON

Tammy Wynette, left, and Jones pose with Miss America 1982 Elizabeth Ward and character actor Slim Pickens during a break in taping for the TV show "Nashville Palace" at Opryland in September 1981.
RICKY ROGERS

Their union produced some emotionally captivating music, including No. 1 hits "We're Gonna Hold On," "Golden Ring" and "Near You," but day-to-day relations were problematic.

Wynette was prone to wrenching melodrama, and Mr. Jones was prone to exacerbating such drama with substance abuse. Once, she hid the keys to his numerous cars to assure that he wouldn't go to town while on a bender. But she neglected to secure the keys to Mr. Jones' riding lawn mower, which he drove to town.

Loretta Lynn warmly introduces Jones when he receives the Music City News Living Legend Award at the Grand Ole Opry House in June 1987. RICK MUSACCHIO

"I was blessed to call George my friend. He was one of the best country singers there ever was."

Loretta Lynn

"I got to my lowest point, where I knew in my thinking that there was no way back at all for me. I'd thrown everything away. ... I tried to put puzzles together to make some way out that could turn out positive. And there was nothing."

George Jones

'I'D THROWN EVERYTHING AWAY'

Mr. Jones and Wynette divorced in 1975, and he found himself at loose ends, driftless and under the influence of drugs and alcohol. Mr. Jones went five years without a No. 1 solo hit after 1975's "The Door" before he entered the studio with producer Sherrill, who wanted him to record a song called "He Stopped Loving Her Today."

"That one was so damn sad that I just didn't think it'd be a hit," Mr. Jones told The Tennessean. "I told Billy Sherrill that, and he said, 'You just trust me. I'm gonna release it. Maybe it's the right time for a sad song.'"

"He Stopped Loving Her Today" became a Grammy Hall of Fame song and a turning point in Mr. Jones' career. He'd earned a reputation as "No Show Jones," a performer likely to be absent from scheduled appearances.

"I got to my lowest point, where I knew in my thinking that there was no way back at all for me," Mr. Jones told The Tennessean. "I'd thrown

Jones poses on the stairs inside George Jones Enterprises, which housed offices and a penthouse, in August 1975 after his divorce from Tammy Wynette. ROBERT JOHNSON

everything away. ... I tried to put puzzles together to make some way out that could turn out positive. And there was nothing."

He was wrong. There was something.

"He Stopped Loving Her Today" was an emotionally captivating triumph that helped restore his place in the industry, and his new relationship with a Louisiana woman named Nancy Sepulvado influenced him to rein in his eccentricities and curb his excesses. In 1983, Nancy Sepulvado became Nancy Jones, and Nancy Jones became the prime factor in calming Mr. Jones' agitations and in smoothing his jagged edges.

Walking through the then-new downtown Country Music Hall of Fame and Museum in 2001, Mr. Jones saw a stage suit on display, and his wife pretended to read from a sign next to the suit.

"It says, 'George Jones was the meanest little thing,'" she said. " 'He has now outgrown all his meanness and is married to the sweetest woman in the world.'"

Mr. Jones had to read the sign for himself before he knew for sure she was joking.

George and Nancy Jones, pictured here on Dec. 8, 2004, put up a huge Christmas display at their Williamson County home for many years. People who showed up to gaze at the lights often left donations for charity. GEORGE WALKER IV

Billy Bob Barnett, left, and Jones discuss their new management agreement over dinner at The Stock-Yard restaurant in July 1981. Barnett, a former pro football player, owned Billy Bob's Texas, a Fort Worth, Texas, nightclub said to be the largest in the world. FRANK EMPSON

NO MORE 'NO SHOW'

"No Show Jones" started to show with regularity, and Mr. Jones' Epic and MCA records of the 1980s and '90s earned radio play. Mr. Jones was inducted into the Country Music Hall of Fame in 1992, and his "I Lived to Tell It All" autobiography became a best-seller in 1996.

No longer a wild-eyed rebel, he became an elder statesman. He was slowed by open-heart surgery in 1994 but had hopes that a move from MCA Records to Asylum would help get his music back on the radio.

But in 1999, while working on his first Asylum album, "The Cold Hard Truth," Mr. Jones crashed his sport-utility vehicle into a bridge near his Franklin, Tenn., home. He had been drinking before the accident, and he suffered a collapsed lung and other serious injuries.

Jones rehearses his song "Choices" on May 1, 2000, preparing for the Academy of Country Music Awards show at Universal City, Calif. ERIC PARSONS

> "The world has lost the greatest country singer of all time. Amen."

Merle Haggard

His new album's first single, "Choices," seemed to address his life's struggles with addiction.

"I've had choices since the day that I was born," he sang. "There were voices that told me right from wrong / If I had listened, no, I wouldn't be here today / Living and dying with the choices I've made."

"Choices" became the final Top 40 country solo hit of Mr. Jones' life, and his vocal performance on it earned him a Grammy Award. The song was nominated for a Country Music Association single of the year, but Mr. Jones was not invited to sing the song in its entirety on the awards show. Alan Jackson, a friend and fan of Mr. Jones, appeared on the show and sang an unscheduled, surprise version of "Choices" that drew a standing ovation.

Mr. Jones had some chart success collaborating with younger artists, singing "Beer Run" with Garth Brooks and "4th of July" with Shooter Jennings, son of Mr. Jones' old friend, Waylon Jennings.

Johnny Paycheck, left, Merle Haggard and Jones perform in the "Workin' Man's Show" on the last day of the 26th annual Fan Fair, June 20, 1997. The show drew an estimated 8,000 to 9,000 fans at the Tennessee State Fairgrounds. RANDY PILAND

From left, Brad Paisley, Bill Anderson, Buck Owens and Jones celebrate Paisley's win for musical event of the year with "Too Country," with vocals by Anderson, Owens and Jones. The honor came during the Country Music Association Awards on Nov. 7, 2001. JOHN PARTIPILO

In the new century, Mr. Jones was vocally supportive of contemporary artists, including Jackson and Kenny Chesney, but was often critical of the pop-leaning sounds he heard on country radio and on awards shows.

"I know things change," he wrote to a Tennessean reporter after viewing a 2001 awards show. "But you would not turn on a classical station to hear rock music, nor would you turn on a jazz station and expect to hear rap music. I believe there is room for all genres of music, and we should hold on to our heritage and make true country music that fans still love."

Fans' love for Mr. Jones was apparent, as he battled chronic hoarseness and respiratory infections through hundreds of sold-out shows during the latter part of his career. Listeners could hear that stress and age had worn away at his voice, but they cheered through concerts that found Mr. Jones working his way through a lifetime of hits.

"It gets into your bronchial tubes, and, Lord, it's just a mess," Mr. Jones

Obviously having a good time, Jones and Dolly Parton crack up after missing their cues while filming a video for their duet, "Blues Man," at the Grand Ole Opry House on Aug. 1, 2005. LARRY McCORMACK

"My heart is absolutely broken. George Jones was my all-time favorite singer and one of my favorite people in the world."

Dolly Parton

Jason Aldean, left, and Jones pose playfully for the cameras on the red carpet before the Nashville Grammy Nominee Party at Loews Vanderbilt Hotel, Jan. 17, 2012. JEANNE REASONOVER

said of singing through congestion.

In 2008, President George W. Bush spoke of Mr. Jones' indelible contributions to American culture while presenting Mr. Jones with a Kennedy Center Honor. And in 2012, Mr. Jones received a Lifetime Achievement Grammy from the Recording Academy.

"I think this is one of the greatest things that can happen to you," he said of his Grammy. "It's not the end of my career, I hope, but we're moving up awful close."

Mr. Jones announced in 2012 that he would embark on a farewell tour in 2013, set to conclude with a Bridgestone Arena concert in Nashville slated for Nov. 22, 2013, featuring guests including Jackson, Kenny Rogers, Garth Brooks, Bobby Bare and many more. But on April 18, Mr. Jones was admitted to Vanderbilt after a routine checkup revealed a fever and irregular blood pressure.

Jones and Reba McEntire bask in the audience's approval after singing "I Was Country When Country Wasn't Cool" for Barbara Mandrell at the Country Music Hall of Fame's Medallion Ceremony, May 17, 2009. MANDY LUNN

"He'll always be the greatest singer and interpreter of country music. There'll never be another."

Alan Jackson

After the announcement of Mr. Jones' death on April 26, other artists surveyed a legacy that drew author Nick Tosches to proclaim, "He is the spirit of country music, plain and simple. It's true Holy Ghost."

"There aren't words in our language to describe the depth of his greatness," said Country Hall of Famer Vince Gill. "I'll miss my kind and generous friend."

Jackson responded, "He'll always be the greatest singer and interpreter of country music. There'll never be another."

Merle Haggard said, "The world has lost the greatest country singer of all time. Amen."

In "The King of Broken Hearts," Jim Lauderdale sang of Mr. Jones, "The King of Broken Hearts is so sad and wise / He can smile while he's crying inside." But in recent years, Mr. Jones was well past crying inside.

"I don't feel that way, not now," he said. "Maybe wiser. But not sad."

Jones poses with a trolley named for him and dedicated at Opryland USA theme park in August 1994. The trolley became part of Nashville's Metro Transit Authority fleet. REX PERRY

Garth Brooks, left, and Jones perform during the 35th annual CMA Awards show at the Grand Ole Opry on Nov. 7, 2001. JOHN PARTIPILO

Perhaps Mr. Jones spent all his sadness on his songs. Perhaps he didn't lend the ache and sorrow to "He Stopped Loving Her Today" and "The Grand Tour." Perhaps that emotion was a gift, not a loan.

"He has a remarkable voice that flows out of him effortlessly and quietly, but with an edge that comes from the story part of the heart," fellow Hall of Famer Emmylou Harris once said of Mr. Jones.

"In the South, we call it high lonesome. I think it's popularly called soul."

GEORGE JONES: THROUGH THE YEARS

George Jones and Tammy Wynette announce Merle Haggard as winner of the album of the year during the CMA Awards ceremonies in 1972. FRANK EMPSON

Sept. 12, 1931
George Jones is born in Saratoga, Texas.

January 1954
Jones cuts his first record in Houston, an original called "No Money in This Deal."

1955
Jones' first top five hit, "Why Baby Why," which he co-wrote, is released.

1959
"White Lightning" becomes Jones' first No. 1 hit.

George Jones accepts the CMA Award for male vocalist of the year, Oct. 12, 1981. RICKY ROGERS

1960s
Jones continues his hit-making streak with songs such as "She Thinks I Still Care," "The Race Is On," "Love Bug," "Walk Through This World With Me" and "A Good Year for the Roses."

1969
Jones marries Tammy Wynette, who became known as the "First Lady of Country Music," with whom he would record over the next decade (even after divorce) classics such as "We're Gonna Hold On," "Golden Ring," "Near You" and "Two Story House."

1975
Jones and Wynette divorce after six years of marriage (Wynette died in April 1998).

1980
Jones' signature song, "He Stopped Loving Her Today," hits No. 1 and becomes his first million seller. The recording also won a Grammy for best male country vocal performance.

1980 and 1981
Jones wins the CMA male vocalist of the year awards.

1983
Jones marries his fourth wife, Nancy Sepulvado, to whom he was married until his death. The marriage became a marker for Jones' rehabilitation from drugs and alcohol, which had prompted troubles that earned him the nickname "No Show Jones" because of canceled appearances.

Nancy and George Jones share a smooch beneath their portrait in their mansion on his 58th birthday, Sept. 12, 1989. ROBERT JOHNSON

ABOVE: Jones shows off his plaque commemorating his induction into the Country Music Hall of Fame during the CMA Awards show Sept. 30, 1992. MIKE DUBOSE

OPPOSITE PAGE: Joe Diffie, right, performs before Jones, left, and Alan Jackson during Jones' 80th birthday celebration at the Grand Ole Opry House, Sept. 13, 2011. SANFORD MYERS

1992
Jones is inducted into the Country Music Hall of Fame.

1996
Autobiography "I Lived to Tell It All" (Villard Books, 1996) is released.

December 2008
Jones is honored in Washington, D.C., as a recipient of the nation's most prominent arts prize, the Kennedy Center Honor, along with Morgan Freeman, Barbra Streisand, Twyla Tharp and Pete Townshend and Roger Daltrey of The Who.

Sept. 12, 2011
Jones turns 80, and the "Grand Ole Opry" celebrates the next night with a tribute concert featuring Alan Jackson, Little Jimmy Dickens, Lee Ann Womack, The Oak Ridge Boys and more.

George Jones, right, was a Lifetime Achievement Award honoree at the 2012 Grammy Awards. He's pictured here with Tom T. Hall at the Nashville Grammy Nominee Party. JEANNE REASONOVER

Feb. 11, 2012
The Recording Academy honors Jones and six other artists with lifetime achievement awards in Los Angeles. On the red carpet, Jones said, "I think this is one of the greatest things that can happen to you. It's not the end of my career, I hope, but we're moving up awful close."

May 26, 2012
Jones is released from his second hospital stay of the year for an upper respiratory infection. He cancels his live performances through June and said in a release he had a new team of doctors treating him, "and it seems to be working." He had spent about a week in the hospital in March as well.

Aug. 14, 2012
Jones, then 80, announces his final tour, named for his hit "The Grand Tour," for 60 cities in 2013.

Nov. 12, 2012
The Country Music Hall of Famer announces that his final show would be at Bridgestone Arena in Nashville on Nov. 22, 2013, as part of his farewell tour. At age 81, Jones said in a news release: "It is tough to stop doing what I love, but the time has come."

Feb. 26, 2013
Garth Brooks is announced as one of a growing list of star performers for the farewell concert. Other performers announced for the show include Alan Jackson, Kid Rock, Kenny Rogers, Randy Travis, Dierks Bentley, Charlie Daniels, Don McLean, Bobby Bare and Barbara Mandrell. Later, more seats are opened for public sale when the final concert becomes a sell-out.

April 18, 2013
Jones is admitted to Vanderbilt University Medical Center in Nashville for observation after a routine checkup that revealed a slight fever and irregular blood pressure.

April 26, 2013
Jones dies at age 81 at Vanderbilt University Medical Center.

May 1, 2013
Friends, family and fellow artists attend a private visitation before Jones' funeral.

May 2, 2013
Jones' funeral is open to the public, and fans pay their respects at the Grand Ole Opry House.

SOURCES: Tennessean archives, Country Music Hall of Fame and Museum, CMA

After Jones' death on April 26, 2013, fans left spontaneous memorials in several places. These roses were left on the steps of Ryman Auditorium, the former home of the Grand Ole Opry, for which Jones frequently performed. SHELLEY MAYS

Loved Ones Say Goodbye

Remembering George Jones the friend, father, husband

By Peter Cooper
The Tennessean | May 1, 2013

Outside Woodlawn-Roesch-Patton Funeral Home this evening, people talked of George Jones as country music's most emotionally eloquent ballad singer. They spoke of Jones' legend, of his soulfulness and of music that will endure beyond the grave.

Inside, away from camera crews and satellite trucks, they spoke more softly.

Outside, they celebrated George Jones' life's work.

Inside, they mourned George Glenn Jones' life, which ended at age 81, on April 26, 2013.

A private visitation for Jones' family and close friends was held at Woodlawn-Roesch-Patton Funeral Home and Memorial Park in Nashville. A far larger public funeral service would be held the following day, but even this visitation drew hundreds; the parking lot overflowed and guests waited in a line out the door to speak with Jones' wife, Nancy, and pay their respects. Among those attending were Jones' colleagues in the country music industry, including Ricky Skaggs, shown here. DIPTI VAIDYA

Inside, they missed a friend. And a father, and a husband.

The following morning would bring a public, televised memorial service for George Jones, with music and testimonials befitting an icon. The private visitation on May 1 was for friends and family — some famed, some anonymous — who laughed gently, or mumbled comfort or choked tears.

I attended the visitation as a journalist, but also as a friendly acquaintance and as a member of the Nashville music community that is lessened by the loss of George Jones.

I won't disrespect a few private hours in a very public death by penning a blow-by-blow of who was there, what they wore and how they acted. And yet people will ask what it was like in there. And I will tell them, and I'll tell you:

Barbara Mandrell, pictured at the private visitation for Jones. DIPTI VAIDYA

Designer Manuel, known for the colorful, heavily ornamented suits he creates for music stars, dresses in somber black for the private visitation for Jones. DIPTI VAIDYA

Brad Paisley arrives at the private visitation for Jones. DIPTI VAIDYA

The Oak Ridge Boys' William Lee Golden attends the private visitation for Jones. DIPTI VAIDYA

John Rich at the private visitation. DIPTI VAIDYA

Tanya Tucker pays her respects. DIPTI VAIDYA

Joe Diffie and Brenda Lee chat outside Jones' visitation. "I was thinking the other day about the song 'Who's Gonna Fill Their Shoes,' and that's never more poignant than now," Lee said. "He was integral to country music." DIPTI VAIDYA

It was just like the visitation held for country music hero Johnny Cash, just like the one for Kitty Wells, and just like the one for Earl Scruggs.

Just like the one for my granddad, who was famous only to his friends.

You've been to these things before. This one was more crowded — with many guests waiting in a two-hour-plus line before greeting the family — but otherwise no different. Visitations are gatherings of people who feel sad and powerless in the wake of death. They are for people who sometimes hug each other without smiling.

They are for coping, not for cheering. And no amount of media hubbub outside the building makes the inside of the building any more or less agonizing than the similar scenes that take place every day, all over our world, in buildings similar and dissimilar. Celebrity has zero to do with tragedy, other than to give it a megaphone.

Larry Gatlin, pictured at the private visitation for Jones. "The man had his demons, but he persevered ... and kept going," Gatlin said. DIPTI VAIDYA

And I'm not suggesting that the death of an 81-year-old man qualifies as tragedy. Certainly, if you'd told Jones at age 50 that he'd live to see 81, he'd have assumed you to be in comic error.

Jones' longevity had a lot to do with the woman at the end of the two-hour line, Nancy Jones, his wife of 30 years who saw past her husband's sins and substances and determined that there was something worth saving in there beyond his honeyed, whiskeyed voice.

It's hard to imagine a job that paid less by the hour than the job of keeping George Jones straight in, say, 1983, but she worked that job tirelessly and, ultimately, effectively. Her work paid off for us, too: We all got three more decades with George Jones the singing star, and with a kinder, more community-minded version of a man who was once a holy terror.

I never knew the howling, outlandish Jones of the 1970s and '80s. I knew a nice old man who was playful around children. I knew a man who worried

Dierks Bentley arrives at Jones' private visitation. DIPTI VAIDYA

about the present and future of the country music industry he'd helped to build, who watched NFL football every autumn Sunday and who delighted in the Christmas lights displayed at the entrance to his and Nancy's Franklin estate. Folks who came to see the lights often made donations to help the less fortunate, and Jones had been less fortunate himself, long ago. He never saw Christmas lights like that, growing up in Vidor, Texas.

I knew a man who clung to his wife like she was his lifeline, mostly because she was his lifeline.

The legendary George Jones, the "King of Broken Hearts," abides. We can listen to him every day, for the rest of our own lives.

But George Glenn Jones, the buddy and daddy, the guy with the great laugh and the ability to talk just like Donald Duck — he's gone now. And hundreds of his friends stood in line on a Wednesday evening for a long time, to tell his wife they were sad about that.

A Song for George

Through laughs and tears, stars offer musical
tribute to the life of their hero

By Peter Cooper
The Tennessean | May 2, 2013

They sang George Jones' life this morning.

They sang his life to mark his death, at a memorial celebration held on the Grand Ole Opry House stage. Singer after singer offered musical tribute to Jones, the master of sad country ballads and the hero to so many musical heroes. And as music rang through the Opry House during the funeral, it became clear that Jones' own life was a joyful song, one of triumph that followed adversity, of peace that followed recklessness.

ABOVE: Brad Paisley performs "Me and Jesus" during Jones' funeral. LARRY McCORMACK

OPPOSITE PAGE: The stage of the Grand Ole Opry House, set for Jones' funeral. Jones sang on that stage many times in his career and once remarked to former Opry announcer Keith Bilbrey that performing at the Opry always made him nervous because he "never got used to" being introduced by his idol, Roy Acuff. LARRY McCORMACK

Jones, who died April 26 at age 81, rarely set pen to paper to rhyme the details of his harrowing descent into addiction and wildness, or of his hard-won redemption. No need. Others had already written his life's song.

"I once was lost, but now am found," sang Jones acolyte Randy Travis.

"Lord, help me, Jesus, I've wasted it/ So help me Jesus, I know what I am," sang Travis Tritt, voicing words from the pen of Kris Kristofferson. "Maybe, Lord, I can show someone else what I've been through myself, on my way back to you."

Brad Paisley was one of numerous performers who spoke of the friendship and kindness Jones displayed in his later years. Paisley chose to memorialize Jones by singing Tom T. Hall's "Me and Jesus."

GEORGE JONES
A Celebration of Life
1931 – 2013

GRANDOLEOPRY

"There aren't words in our language to describe the depth of his greatness. I'll miss my kind and generous friend."

Vince Gill, on the day of Jones' death

"I know a man who once was a sinner," Paisley sang. "I know a man that once was a drunk/ I know a man who once was a loser/ He went out one day and made an altar out of a stump."

Many at the service credited Jones' widow, Nancy, with steering him through his recovery and with adding three decades to a life that seemed at risk when Jones was in his 50s.

She wept as Vince Gill struggled to rein in his own emotions, singing his own "Go Rest High On That Mountain."

"I know your life on earth was troubled," Gill sang. "And only you could know the pain/ You weren't afraid to face the devil, you were no stranger to the rain." Patty Loveless joined Gill for the exultant chorus: "Go rest high on that mountain, son, your work on earth is done/ Go to heaven a'shoutin'."

The memorial at the 4,400-seat Opry House included music from Gill, Loveless, Travis, Paisley, Tritt, the Oak Ridge Boys, Charlie Daniels, Kid Rock, Ronnie Milsap, Wynonna Judd, Alan Jackson and Tanya Tucker with the Imperials, as well as spoken tributes from former first lady of the United States Laura Bush, Kenny Chesney, CBS chief Washington correspondent Bob Schieffer, Opry General Manager Pete Fisher, Tennessee Gov. Bill Haslam, former Arkansas Gov. Mike Huckabee, pastor Mike Wilson and Jones' fellow Country Music Hall of Famer Barbara Mandrell.

ABOVE: Vince Gill chokes up while singing "Go Rest High On That Mountain" with Patty Loveless during Jones' funeral service. LARRY McCORMACK

BELOW: Vince Gill, with Patty Loveless by his side, does an instrumental solo while composing himself. LARRY McCORMACK

PHOTO ON PRECEDING PAGE: A tearful Alan Jackson caps Jones' funeral by singing Jones' most famous song, "He Stopped Loving Her Today." LARRY McCORMACK

An emotional Barbara Mandrell speaks of her friendship with Jones during his funeral. LARRY McCORMACK

"I believe if you ask any singer who was the greatest country music singer of all time, they would say 'George Jones.' He was without question and by far the best! I first met and worked with him when I was 13 years old; I am so very grateful that he was my friend."

Barbara Mandrell, reacting to the news of Jones' death

Though most famous faces in attendance at Jones' funeral hailed from the country music industry, several represented the political world. Tennessee Gov. Bill Haslam is pictured here speaking during the service. Former first lady of the United States Laura Bush also spoke, as did former Arkansas Gov. Mike Huckabee.
LARRY McCORMACK

Wynonna Judd sang "How Great Thou Art." She had to wipe away tears.
LARRY McCORMACK

Former first lady of the United States Laura Bush spoke at Jones' funeral, mentioning that former President George W. Bush liked to work out to Jones' hit "White Lightning." A Texas native like Jones, she said, "We've heard few sounds more lovely than the voice of George Jones." LARRY McCORMACK

Garth Brooks gives a hug at the Grand Ole Opry House on the day of Jones' funeral service.
LARRY McCORMACK

"When I interviewed him back in 2009, I came away feeling like his whole life was a surprise to him, and he never quite believed any of it."

CBS News correspondent Bob Schieffer, speaking at Jones' funeral. LARRY McCORMACK

ABOVE: Tanya Tucker and The Imperials sang "Old Rugged Cross," opening Jones' funeral before the crowd at the Grand Ole Opry House.
LARRY McCORMACK

RIGHT: Jones' portrait graces the stage during his funeral. The butterfly floral arrangement to the right was sent by Dolly Parton.
LARRY McCORMACK

Thousands of fans crowded the Opry Plaza for a chance to sit in the balcony during the public funeral. Some camped overnight, and hundreds were there by 6 a.m.

The Opry balcony was not large enough to accommodate the flood of people, some in sober business suits, others in cowboy hats and old Jones T-shirts. The Opry House's lower level was mostly filled with grieving friends, but the emotion in the balcony was no less real or connected.

These were people who sought a way to express their love for Jones' music, and for a man they took as the living embodiment of the songs he sang.

One woman said her brother used to clean Jones' pool, and a 22-year-old Middle Tennessee State University student who sings and writes songs called Jones his biggest influence. A 76-year-old woman said she shouted gleefully when she received a ticket the prior Christmas for what was to be Jones' retirement concert in November 2013 in Nashville, and that she cried upon hearing of Jones' death. A man drove through the night from Tabor, Iowa, to, he said, "Pay my respects and say, 'Thank you.'"

Jones' casket was covered in white flowers, as WSM and Grand Ole Opry announcer Eddie Stubbs offered opening remarks and brought out Tucker and The Imperials to sing the hymn, "Old Rugged Cross." Stubbs shared announcing duties with former Opry announcer and close Jones friend Keith Bilbrey, who recalled that Jones told him that the only time he was nervous about singing was on the stage of the Grand Ole Opry.

"I said, 'What about the Opry makes you nervous?' He said, 'Roy Acuff,'" Bilbrey remarked. Jones grew up listening to the Opry, and if he fell asleep during the show his mother would wake him when Acuff came on.

"He said, 'I never get used to standing on that stage, and I never get used to Roy Acuff introducing me,'" Bilbrey said. "We revere and idolize George Jones, but he, too, had his idols."

Nancy Jones, front row, second from left, flanked by family members, watches as George Jones' casket is moved from the Grand Ole Opry House to a waiting hearse. SHELLEY MAYS

Jones' public funeral attracted not only his oldest fans, but also some young children. SHELLEY MAYS

"Like me, I'm sure music fans around the world can't get 'He Stopped Loving Her Today' out of their head on this sad day. Nashville has lost a legend. When I moved to Nashville in 1978, one of the first places I visited was George's Possum Holler nightclub. It was a great introduction to Nashville. Our thoughts and prayers are with his wife, Nancy, his family and his dear friends."

Nashville Mayor Karl Dean, in a statement issued upon Jones' death

One fan uses the title of Jones' signature song scrawled on a truck window to pay tribute. SHELLEY MAYS

ABOVE: This fan was one of many who felt the urge to touch Jones' image on a sign posted outside the Opry House while awaiting his funeral. SHELLEY MAYS

BELOW: Josh Owens of Kentucky awaits Jones' funeral services bearing roses for Jones' wife and daughter. SHELLEY MAYS

ABOVE: Jones' funeral, held at the Grand Ole Opry House in Nashville on May 2, 2013, was open to the public. Thousands of fans waited hours – some of them overnight – in a line snaking along sidewalks surrounding the Opry House for a chance to pay their respects. The 4,400-seat concert venue couldn't accommodate everyone, so some people outside listened to the service's audio, broadcast from inside. SHELLEY MAYS

PHOTO ON PRECEDING PAGE: Ronnie Milsap performs "When the Grass Grows Over Me" during Jones' funeral. LARRY McCORMACK

Schieffer grew up in Jones' native Texas, listening to Jones on the Opry.

"Everybody wanted to sing like George Jones," Schieffer said. "But nobody could sing like George Jones unless you were George Jones. You couldn't, because you hadn't been through what he had been through. When I interviewed him back in 2009, I came away feeling like his whole life was a surprise to him, and he never quite believed any of it."

Daniels and Gill each talked about the futility of attempting to sing like Jones, whose phrasing and fluidity set him apart from his predecessors and those who came up under his influence.

"With young singers that tried to emulate George Jones, it was an affectation," Daniels said, while Gill recalled the days when he himself possessed that affectation. He was a young artist in the recording studio when producer Emory Gordy Jr. halted the session:

"He said, 'We already have a George Jones,'" Gill remembered. " 'You need to find a way to sing like you.'" Gill soon found a way to do so, and he's now a member of the Country Music Hall of Fame.

A woman leaves flowers as she makes her way into Jones' funeral. SHELLEY MAYS

Margie Lee, of Chicago, bears a photo, taken at a Jones concert in 1966, of her hugging the country star. Lee waited with thousands of others to attend Jones' public memorial. LARRY McCORMACK

Jones' fans, weeping and wielding cameras, watch from behind a gate as his casket is carried from the Grand Ole Opry House to a waiting hearse. SHELLEY MAYS

ABOVE: Jones' casket is rolled past thousands of mourners at the conclusion of his funeral at the Grand Ole Opry House. LARRY McCORMACK

OPPOSITE PAGE: A hearse leads a long funeral procession of cars leaving the Grand Ole Opry House, headed for Nashville's Woodlawn Memorial Park for Jones' burial, May 2, 2013. STEVEN S. HARMAN

Another Hall of Famer, Garth Brooks, sat next to the former first lady in the front row, but did not appear onstage. He and wife Trisha Yearwood stood repeatedly, following the emotional musical performances.

Bush relayed greetings from her husband, former U.S. President George W. Bush, and from her father-in-law, former President George H.W. Bush. She also spoke of playing Jones' songs on jukeboxes when she was a teenager.

"Pain and love: George Jones spoke of both of them whenever he sang a note," Bush said. "In American music, George was truly a legend beyond compare. As for me, I've been very lucky to walk through this world with my own George. And in that walk, we've heard few sounds more lovely than the voice of George Jones."

Mandrell, whose hit song "I Was Country (When Country Wasn't Cool)" featured a guest vocal from Jones, spoke of Jones' unprecedented and un-equaled way with a song.

Ann Kelley, of Smyrna, Tenn., pays her respects at Jones' gravesite at Nashville's Woodlawn Memorial Park, May 2, 2013. SHELLEY MAYS

"A supremely magnificent, unparalleled, one-of-a-kind voice," she said. "George was and always will be the greatest singer of all time."

Several speakers made reference to Jones' ex-wife and duet partner, Tammy Wynette. Tritt said he was on a movie set in Spain with Kristofferson when Wynette died in 1998.

"I said, 'With all the years of hard living that George had, who would have ever thought that he would outlive Tammy,'" Tritt said. "Kris looked at me and said, 'Had it not been for Nancy, he would not have.' George said it many times: 'She's my angel, and she saved my life.'"

That life was celebrated, and sung, over a remarkable two hours and 40 minutes, as morning stretched into afternoon. The service reached its climax as Jackson sang Jones' signature song, the Bobby Braddock- and Curly Putman-written "He Stopped Loving Her Today."

"They placed a wreath upon his door," Jackson sang, through tears. "And soon they'll carry him away. He stopped loving her today."

And then they carried him away, leaving his friends and his family and his fans to cry and smile, to listen and to remember.

"He knew about heartbreak. He knew about disappointment," Schieffer said. "He knew about betrayal. He was more than a country singer. He was a country song."

He knew about more than heartbreak, disappointment and betrayal, though. He knew redemption and steadfast love.

Yes, he was a country song.

A joyful one, at that.

On Dec. 7, 2008, George Jones was awarded a Kennedy Center Honor, the nation's top prize in the arts, in a glittering, celebrity-studded ceremony at the John F. Kennedy Center for the Performing Arts in Washington, D.C.

The Tennessean's music columnist, Peter Cooper, was on hand to witness the effusive accolades for Jones that night, some of them from surprising sources.

National Recognition and Praise

Kennedy Center Honors celebrate George Jones' life, music

By Peter Cooper
The Tennessean | Dec. 7, 2008

With a rainbow-colored ribbon around his neck signifying his position as a Kennedy Center Honoree, George Jones paused for a moment on Sunday evening.

He stood on the most surreal red carpet in America — earlier, that carpet had been crushed under the feet of Speaker of the House of Representatives Nancy Pelosi, former Speaker Newt Gingrich, former Wonder Woman Lynda Carter and the R&B musician who goes by the

> "George has probably influenced more country artists than anyone that's ever been in this business, or ever will be."

Randy Travis

stage name Ne-Yo — and pondered a weekend spent amidst Washington power players and fellow honorees Morgan Freeman, Barbra Streisand, Twyla Tharp and Pete Townshend and Roger Daltrey of The Who.

"We've met some beautiful people, and they kind of feel like old friends," said Jones, who at 77 is largely acknowledged as possessing the greatest singing voice in country music history. "We met Aretha Franklin, and she's real nice. And Barbra Streisand, she's just right down to earth. Barbra's husband, James Brolin, he's just about as country as you're going to get. I mean, he loves country music. I'm very surprised that so many of them are familiar with my work."

Jones' wife, Nancy, then advised as to how she was going to have to crack the whip around their house over the holidays to keep Jones' head from a perma-swell, given all the kind words directed his way in Washington during the nation's most prominent annual arts celebration.

Caroline Kennedy praised his "tear-stained voice and raw emotion." Laura Bush introduced the Jones tribute section of the Honors by saying that she and her husband "have heard few sounds more lovely than the voice of George Jones. It's a beautiful gift to the world." Lily Tomlin professed her fandom, Alan Jackson called Jones "the last great voice of real country music," and Randy Travis said, "George has probably influenced more country artists than anyone that's ever been in this business, or ever will be."

Jones' official tribute included versions of his songs from Travis, Garth Brooks, Jackson and Brad Paisley, and a stirring version of "Amazing Grace" from Shelby Lynne, whom Jones took under his wing when she was a teenager. That gospel song was a nod to Jones' love of religious music and to his own life story, which involved plenty of shenanigans on the way to late-life sobriety.

Thirty years ago, Jones would have been cowed by the notion of sitting in starched clothes under chandeliers that snaked and gleamed like the rhinestone design on some giant's Manuel suit, in between a president and a movie star. All that would have been more than enough incentive for Jones to get bombed out of his skull, miss another plane and give another reason for folks to call him "No Show Jones" instead of his more respectable nickname of "Possum."

Somehow, though, Jones seemed perfectly in place throughout the evening. As ambassadors and A-list celebrities, senators and statesmen found their seats, the sound system played Streisand's elegant version of "Somewhere" and The Who's nearly operatic "Love, Reign O'er Me," and then there were piano tinkles and a honky-tonk beat and a Bible Belt voice that sounded at home inside the Capital Beltway: "In North Carolina, way back in the hills/ Lived my old pappy and he had him a still," began the recording of Jones' "White Lightning."

The official program began with host Kennedy's welcome, and with some video from a Sunday afternoon White House ceremony. At that meeting, outspoken Bush critic Streisand met the outgoing president for the first time, and their cheek-peck was surely the most uncomfortable screen kiss of her career: The apparently recession-proof Kennedy Center audience — some of the 2,300 audience members had paid as much as $4,000 for tickets — guffawed at the footage. Jones and Bush eschewed comedic possibilities and opted for a handshake.

Then the tributes started, with Denzel Washington and Clint Eastwood talking about Tennessee native Freeman, who basked in blues performances from artists including 80-year-old Koko Taylor, 93-year-old Honeyboy Edwards, 95-year-old Pinetop Perkins and 83-year-old B.B. King. Daltrey and Townshend's segment was next, and that one featured music from Dave Grohl, Bettye LaVette, Rob Thomas and Chris Cornell, as well as a riotous introduction from actor Jack Black, who praised The Who for "a collection of ass-kicking songs the likes of which will never be seen again."

Dancer and choreographer Twyla Tharp's portion of the evening involved intricate, flowing movements that in no way resembled the stuff that Jones has seen a thousand times from, say, the Melvin Sloan Dancers at the Grand Ole Opry. And major stars — Beyonce, Glenn Close and Queen Latifah — participated in the Streisand section.

Jones' moment came after the intermission, just prior to Streisand's show-ending tribute. President Bush, who earlier had thumbed distractedly through a souvenir calendar while Kennedy spoke, appeared energized and enthused about Jones: He mouthed the words to "The Race Is On" while Brooks sang, and several times he patted Jones on the back good-naturedly.

Laura Bush spoke for several minutes about Jones' legacy and "one-of-a-kind voice," and then a video aired that documented Jones' artistic triumphs and personal struggles.

"We're celebrating his life," Honors producer George Stevens Jr. said during a rehearsal. "And so first we want to tell his story, and to do it with a certain grace."

Paisley played and sang a version of Jones' hit, "Bartender's Blues," and Travis introduced his take on "One Woman Man" by saying, "The Lord only made one George Jones ... Probably thought, 'That's enough. Better stop right there.'"

Jones seemed thrilled by Jackson's restrained, respectful "He Stopped Loving Her Today," and Brooks performed what the script referred to as "The Possum Medley:" "White Lightning," "The Grand Tour" and "The Race Is On."

Lynne's "Amazing Grace" concluded the Possum portion, and thousand-dollar dresses rose from $4,000 seats as Jones received a standing ovation without having to sing a note. He smiled and waved there in the presidential box, looking at once regal and just as down to earth as ... his new pal Barbra Streisand. George Jones was 700 miles from home and years removed from many dangers, toils and snares.

A Life in Music

The Tennessean's
photographers bore
witness to Jones,
on and off stage

Jones stars at the
CBS Records show
on Oct. 21, 1978.
S.A. TARKINGTON

Jones, left, and his wife at the time, Tammy Wynette, right, chat with Mario Ferrari at his restaurant, Mario's, in January 1970. Jones and Wynette were one of the hottest acts in Nashville during their marriage. BILL PRESTON

Dolly Parton, left, and Barbara Mandrell announce Jones as the male vocalist of the year at the CMA Awards show at the Grand Ole Opry House on Oct. 13, 1980. They accepted the award for him, too; Jones didn't attend the ceremony.
RICKY ROGERS

Jones performs for a small crowd at an outdoor concert at Pee Wee restaurant and nightclub in West Nashville on Aug. 1, 1982. RICKY ROGERS

Melba Montgomery joins Jones during a benefit concert on Dec. 9, 1982, for the 100 Club. Montgomery and Jones were a major country duet team in the mid-'60s and they reprised their biggest hit, "We Must Have Been Out of Our Minds." DAN LOFTIN

ABOVE: Jones and Randy Travis exchange songs and stories at a taping session for an HBO special, "Influences." Some 300 fans crowded into Zanies Comedy Night Club as Scene Three Inc. taped the hour-long special on Aug. 27, 1991. ROBERT JOHNSON

LEFT: Jones prepares for a pitch during the Fan Fair celebrity softball tournament at Greer Stadium on June 6, 1993. MIKE DUBOSE

ABOVE: On Jan. 22, 1991, Jones hosted a reception at his home for renegade star Johnny Paycheck, left, who was released from prison 10 days earlier after serving two years for shooting a man in an Ohio bar in 1985. Here Paycheck chats with Tom T. Hall, center, and Jones. BILL STEBER

LEFT: Jones and Johnny Paycheck share a moment during the party at Jones' home. Jones lent Paycheck some help after Paycheck's release from prison by recording a duet with him called "The Last Outlaw is Alive and Doing Well." BILL STEBER

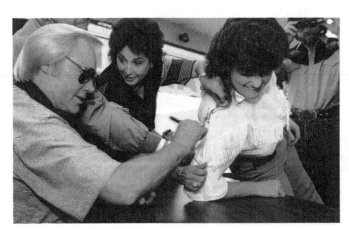

Jones gets help from his wife, Nancy, in autographing Franklin, Tenn., resident Margaret Dickens' shirt. Fans crowded the Harpeth Jeep dealership on March 29, 1997, to meet Jones and register for a chance to win an autographed guitar.
PEYTON HOGE

LEFT: Jones makes his way past celebrities including Marty Stuart, left, Vince Gill and Reba McEntire, heading for the stage at the opening of the TNN Music City News Country Awards show on June 7, 1993. DELORES DELVIN

Jones and his former wife and singing partner, Tammy Wynette, in April 1995 announce "One," their reunion album, to be released by MCA, and an accompanying tour. RICK MUSACCHIO

Jones relaxes at Mt. Juliet recording studio Bradley's Barn during a February 1994 session with some friends, including Ricky Skaggs, right. FREEMAN RAMSEY

Trinity Elementary School's marquee displays a get-well message for Jones on March 9, 1999, three days after he wrecked his sport-utility vehicle near the school. The students also signed an oversized greeting card. SHELLEY MAYS

ABOVE LEFT: Jones appears in Williamson County court in Franklin, Tenn., on May 12, 1999, to plead guilty to charges of driving while impaired and violating the state open-container law, stemming from his car wreck two months earlier. A reckless driving charge would be dismissed if Jones completed alcohol counseling and went a year without another arrest. SHELLEY MAYS

ABOVE RIGHT: Jones, lower center in a purple shirt, faces a throng of reporters outside the Williamson County courthouse after his hearing. SHELLEY MAYS

Jones' appearance at the Asylum Records show on the first day of the 28th annual Fan Fair at the Tennessee State Fairgrounds on June 14, 1999, was his first Nashville performance after his car crash three months earlier. JACKIE BELL

Jones, left, performs "Golden Ring" with his daughter, Georgette Smith, in Andalusia, Ala., on June 5, 1999. It was Jones' first show since his near-fatal auto wreck three months earlier, and his first duet with his daughter in 18 years. JARED LAZARUS

Jones appears at the Wal-Mart store in Franklin in June 1999 for an autograph session, part of promotions efforts for a new album, "Cold Hard Truth." A huge crowd turns out to meet him. Jesse Sober, left, of Atlanta, asks Jones to sign his guitar, festooned with other music stars' autographs. JOHN PARTIPILO

Jones attended a CD release party at Sound Kitchen Studios in Nashville in July 1999 to celebrate a new album by "Queen of Gospel Music" Vestal Goodman.

ABOVE: Jones and Dolly Parton crack up during the party. The two sang on Goodman's duets album, "Vestal & Friends." Seated beside Jones is his granddaughter, Breann Hohimer. BILL STEBER

LEFT: Jones, second from right, joins in singing "Amazing Grace" with gospel star Andraé Crouch on piano, and, from left, Carman, Jake Hess, Dolly Parton and Goodman. BILL STEBER

Jones performs at Ryman Auditorium, Aug. 27, 1999. RANDY PILAND

From left, Crystal Gayle, Jones, Loretta Lynn and Naomi Judd pose during the grand opening of the
Loretta Lynn Hurricane Mills Museum on May 26, 2001. FREEMAN RAMSEY

Country Music Hall of Fame director Kyle Young, left, accompanies Jones on a preview tour of the Hall's new $37 million building in May 2001. ERIC PARSONS

Little Jimmy Dickens, left, and Jones enjoy the activities during the grand opening of the new Country Music Hall of Fame and Museum on May 17, 2001. BILL STEBER

Jones gives a thumbs-up to a banner held by former members of Johnny Paycheck's band as he approaches the burial site for his friend at Nashville's Woodlawn cemetery, Feb. 25, 2003. BILL STEBER

Jones sings "He Stopped Loving Her Today" at the 100th Birthday Show for Nashville Association of Musicians on Oct. 7, 2002, at the Grand Ole Opry House.
P. CASEY DALEY

ABOVE: Kris Kristofferson, left, Willie Nelson and Jones play together during the Johnny Cash Memorial Tribute at Ryman Auditorium on Nov. 10, 2003. BILL STEBER

OPPOSITE PAGE: Jones took the stage during his 75th birthday tribute at the Grand Ole Opry, Sept. 12, 2006. MICHAEL CLANCY

Country stars often gathered to pay tribute to Jones' birthdays. Here, Jones hails the crowd from the Grand Ole Opry stage, with his wife, Nancy, on the left, and Tanya Tucker, Joe Nichols and Dierks Bentley on the right, during his 75th birthday event on Sept. 12, 2006. MICHAEL CLANCY

Jones and Nancy cheer for Billy Ray Cyrus. MICHAEL CLANCY

LEFT: Little Jimmy Dickens, left, shakes hands with Jones as Joe Diffie and Craig Morgan look on.
MICHAEL CLANCY

BELOW: Jones took the stage during the celebration.
MICHAEL CLANCY

Jones signs autographs for fans upon arrival at the Country Music Hall of Fame, May 6, 2007.
SHAUNA BITTLE

Jones performs as part of the Musicians Hall of Fame Awards show at the Schermerhorn Symphony
Center in Nashville, on Nov. 26, 2007. MANDY LUNN

Jones gets a surprise birthday party at Logan's Roadhouse in the Cool Springs, Tenn., on Sept, 12, 2007. STEVEN S. HARMAN

Country music star Trace Adkins, right, greets Jones at his surprise 76th birthday party. STEVEN S. HARMAN

LEFT: Jones laughs as Jimmy Dickens has some fun with the crowd during Jones' 80th birthday celebration at the Grand Ole Opry House on Sept. 13, 2011. SANFORD MYERS

BELOW: Dusty King, left, and Karen Oliver, of Ontario, Canada, pause outside the front gate of Jones' Franklin home shortly after his death on April 26, 2013. The fans, visiting Nashville that day, left flowers at the gate.
MARK ZALESKI

CREDITS

GEORGE JONES: KING OF BROKEN HEARTS
was produced by the staff of The Tennessean:

Maria De Varenne, Executive Editor and Vice President/News
Meg Downey, Managing Editor
Linda Zettler, Lifestyles and Entertainment Editor
Tom Stanford, Visuals Editor
Maura Ammenheuser, Book Production Editor
Michael Babin and **Krista Volenski Wilcox**, Design Team Leaders
Ricky Rogers, Photo Researcher

Written by Peter Cooper

Photographers: Larry McCormack, Jackie Bell, Kats Barry,
Shauna Bittle, Michael Clancy, P. Casey Daley, Delores Delvin,
Mike DuBose, Frank Empson, Dale Ernsberger, Steven S. Harman,
Peyton Hoge, Robert Johnson, Jared Lazarus, Dan Loftin, Mandy Lunn,
Shelley Mays, Rick Musacchio, Sanford Myers, Eric Parsons, John Partipilo,
Rex Perry, Randy Piland, Bill Preston, Freeman Ramsey, Jeanne Reasonover,
Ricky Rogers, Bill Steber, S.A. Tarkington, Dipti Vaidya, George Walker IV,
Nancy Warnecke, Mark Zaleski

Copy editors: Craig Flagg, Heather Fritz Aronin, Karen Grigsby

CPSIA information can be obtained at www.ICGtesting.com
Printed in the USA
LVOW02s0325011013

354843LV00004B/4/P